contents

GRAMMAR RAY

ADVERBS

a graphic guide to grammar

andrew carter

Evans

Published by Evans Brothers Limited
2A Portman Mansions
Chiltern Street
London W1U 6NR

© in this edition Evans Brothers Limited 2010
© in the text and illustrations Andrew Carter 2010

Printed in Malta by Gutenberg Press

Editor: Nicola Edwards
Designer: Mark Holt

British Library Cataloguing in Publication Data

Carter, Andrew.
Adverbs. — (Grammar Ray)
1. English language—Adverb—Juvenile literature.I.
Title II. Series
425.7'6-dc22

ISBN-13: 9780237538507

VISIT OUR WEBSITE
Evans
www.evansbooks.co.uk

INTRODUCTION

Hello and welcome to Grammar Ray! You are
about to enter a world of fun and adventure, where
English grammar is brought to life. Words in the English
language can be divided into different groups called
'parts of speech'. In this title, we will join the
robots in their quest to explore the
role of the adverb.

I'm Verb-Man. Join me as I fight Grammevil,
my deadliest enemy, and his army of killer
verb-bots for control of Adverbia.

The first part of the book is a comic strip.
Join Verb-Man in his fight for control over the
power of Adverbia. Can he defeat Grammevil
and his army of killer verb-bots? Look
out for the words in purple - they
are key to the story.

After you've followed Verb-Man's adventures,
the rest of the book looks at adverbs in more
detail, and gives some more examples. Use this if
you need a reminder of the role adverbs play in
English grammar. It also requires your puzzle-
solving skills, and tests what you have learnt
along the way. So be sure to pay attention!

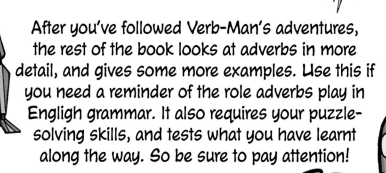

Let's revise verbs and adjectives

An adverb is a word that gives us information about a verb (and sometimes about an adjective). Let's look at what we know about verbs and adjectives.

Verbs are the words we use to describe physical and mental actions:

to fly

to read

Adjectives describe nouns. They tell us about things such as colour, quantity, size and personality:

a small, white rabbit

a greedy, hungry hare

What do adverbs do?

Adverbs can give information about <u>how</u> a verb happens. For example, by adding an adverb to the verb 'to read' we can find out if someone is reading slowly, excitedly or carefully.

Adverbs can also tell us about <u>when</u> and <u>where</u> something happens, for example: now, later, always, here, there, everywhere.

Let's look at some examples in the latest issue of Verb-Man...

GR COMICS

R 50
no.156

THE INCREDIBLE ADVENTURES OF

VERB→MAN

VERB - MAN'S
DEADLIEST ENEMY
FINALLY RETURNS...

AND A NEW POWER IS AMAZINGLY REVEALED!

0 01237 518

Deep in Antarctica, Verb-Man and his trusted companion Vanessa are searching expectantly for the mythical, lost city of Adverbia.

Look there!

The map tells me that the entrance should be somewhere near here.

Verb-Man points excitedly at something through the blizzard.

soon

Soon we can rejoin the two halves of the legendary Adverbian amulet.

The gateway to Adverbia!

Bravely, the two explorers step into the temple.

"Look at that statue!"

Beside the intricately painted hieroglyphics sits something amazing.

Beside

"My father gave me the half of the amulet that was in his museum."

"There is the missing half of the amulet!"

"Verb-Man, put the halves back together and make the amulet complete again."

Vanessa's pet otter suddenly senses something!

It can't be!

A strange figure is laughing manically.

Yes, Verb-Man, it is I, your arch-enemy Professor B. Grammevil! I followed you here with my killer verb-bots and soon I will take the power of Adverbia for myself!

This time you cannot stop me, Verb-Man. My killer verb-bots are equal to your powers and each has its own special ability...

They can electrocute, freeze, burn, and fight!

DESTROY HIM!

TARGET ACQUIRED

TARGET ACQUIRED

My only chance is to complete the amulet.

Verb-Man is backed dangerously into a corner.

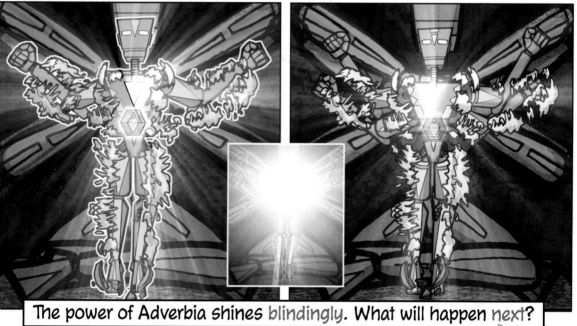

The power of Adverbia shines blindingly. What will happen next?

I've been completely transformed!

Nooo! The power of Adverbia must be mine!

Verb-bots, eliminate him!

13

You cannot stop me *now*, Grammevil! With the power of Adverbia I can...

fly quickly,

TARGET ACQUIRED

move incredibly fast...

SWOOSH

SMACK

and *hit* very hard!

Your verb-bots are *good*...

Adverbs are also often used with adjectives.

FSSSSSS

just not...

TARGET ACQUIRED

good enough!

Noooooo!

14

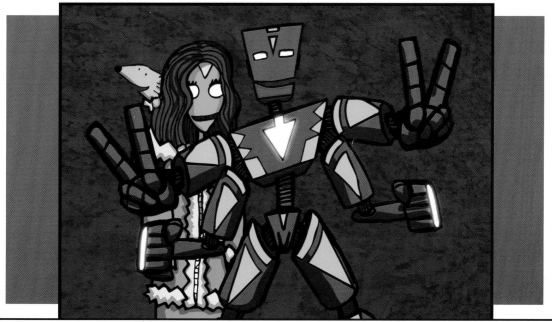

Our heroes have triumphed *again*, but has Grammevil *truly* been defeated?

Adverbs

An adverb is a word that we commonly use to give more information about a verb.

FOR EXAMPLE:

run <u>quickly</u>   *think <u>deeply</u>*
(VERB) (ADVERB)   (VERB) (ADVERB)

We can also use an adverb to give more information about an adjective:

FOR EXAMPLE:

It is a <u>very</u> hungry rabbit.
(ADVERB) (ADJECTIVE)

It was an <u>extremely</u> large verb-bot.
(ADVERB) (ADJECTIVE)

We usually form adverbs by adding -ly to adjectives:

FOR EXAMPLE:

The sad robot trudged down the road.
(ADJECTIVE)

The robot trudged <u>sadly</u> down the road.
(ADVERB)

Not all adverbs end in -ly though:

FOR EXAMPLE:

Verb-Man ran up the wall <u>fast</u>.

And not all words that end in -ly are adverbs!

FOR EXAMPLE:

There's an <u>ugly fly</u> on that <u>lovely</u> bunch of flowers!

It is sometimes easy to get an adverb confused with an adjective:

FOR EXAMPLE:

He swims slow.   (incorrect - 'slow' is an adjective)

He swims <u>slowly</u>.   (correct - 'slowly' is an adverb)

We use an adverb to describe a verb and an adjective to describe a noun:

FOR EXAMPLE:	*a slow swimmer* (ADJECTIVE) (NOUN)

Sometimes an adjective and an adverb can be the same:

FOR EXAMPLE:	*She jumped <u>high</u>.* *a <u>high</u> building* (VERB) (ADVERB) (ADJECTIVE) (NOUN)

Adverbs can tell us about when, where and how something is happening:

When:

FOR EXAMPLE:	*She <u>always</u> hands in her homework on time.* *He <u>never</u> remembers his football kit.* *They <u>sometimes</u> visit their grandparents at the weekend.*

Where:

FOR EXAMPLE:	*Come <u>here</u>!* *Run over <u>there</u>.* *There are flies <u>everywhere</u>!*

How:

FOR EXAMPLE:	*Grammevil was acting <u>suspiciously</u>.* *Verb-Man fought <u>bravely</u>.* *Vanessa studied the map <u>carefully</u>.*

Adverb phrases

An adverb phrase is a group of words in a sentence that we can use like an adverb to tell us more about a verb.

First let us look at some sentences with adverbs in them:

FOR EXAMPLE:

Verb-Man flew <u>quickly</u>.

This sentence uses the adverb '<u>quickly</u>' and tells us how fast Verb-Man flew.

FOR EXAMPLE:

<u>Formerly</u> there was a wise, old king.

In this sentence the adverb '<u>formerly</u>' tells us when there was a wise, old king.

Now let us look at the same sentences using an adverb phrase:

FOR EXAMPLE:

Verb-Man flew <u>faster than a bullet</u>.

This sentence uses the adverb phrase '<u>faster than a bullet</u>' like a single adverb to tell us exactly how quickly Verb-Man flew.

FOR EXAMPLE:

<u>Once upon a time</u> there was a wise, old king.

In this sentence the adverb phrase '<u>Once upon a time</u>' acts like the single adverb 'formerly' to tell us when there was a wise, old king.

phrasal verbs

**A phrasal verb is a verb combined with prepositions or adverbs.
The meaning of a phrasal verb is different from that of the words it consists of.**

Let us look at some examples in this profile of Verb-Man's enemy Phearasal:

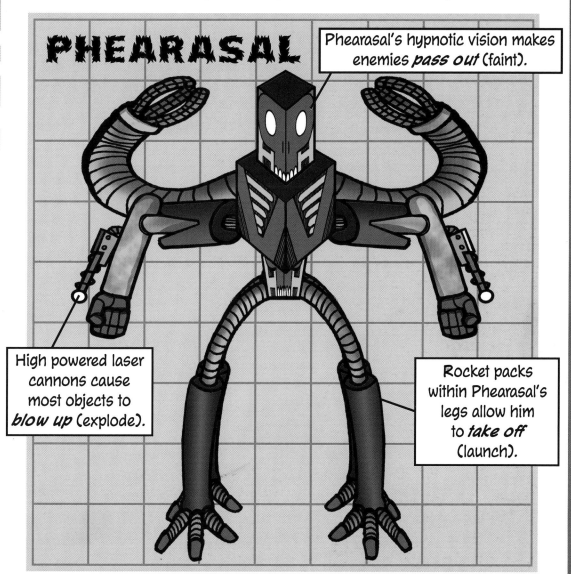

PHEARASAL

Phearasal's hypnotic vision makes enemies *pass out* (faint).

High powered laser cannons cause most objects to *blow up* (explode).

Rocket packs within Phearasal's legs allow him to *take off* (launch).

Phearasal's origin is shrouded in mystery and he is Verb-Man's most mysterious foe. The two have ***come up against*** each other on numerous occasions and Verb-Man has often had to ***deal with*** Phearasal ***breaking into*** high security banks and research facilities. Despite being ***locked up*** several times, Phearasal has always managed to ***break out*** within days.

adverbs
test yourself

1. Which two of these parts of speech can adverbs describe?

adjectives   nouns   prepositions   pronouns   verbs

2. Which adverb is the odd one out in the following lists of time and place adverbs?

(a) here, near, sometimes, somewhere
(b) now, always, often, nowhere

3. Which words in the sentences are adverbs?

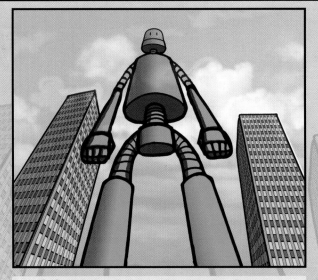

(a) It is a very tall, green robot.
(b) The cat can jump high.
(c) She quickly cleaned the car.

MIRACLE HAIR GROWTH

INSTANT RESULTS

HAIR GRO

BEFORE APPLYING   AFTER APPLYING

Our Miracle Hair Gro Formula starts working instantly*. Simply apply our patented formula daily and your hair will grow quickly and shine brightly. Send R20 today for your first bottle of Miracle Gro and we'll send you a FREE comb.

MIRACLE GRO CO. BOX 22456
NEW VERB CITY

*Miracle Hair Gro may take 10-30 years before best results are seen.

4. Identify nine adverbs in the advert above.

5. Match the following phrasal verbs to their meanings.

A. go off   1. increase the volume

B. look into   2. surrender

C. give up   3. explode

D. turn up   4. investigate

21

1. verbs and adjectives

2. (a) 'sometimes' describes when and the others describe where
(b) 'nowhere' describes where and the others describe when

3. (a) very, (b) high, (c) quickly

4. 'BEFORE', 'AFTER', 'instantly', 'simply', 'daily', 'quickly', 'brightly', 'today', 'before'

5. A-3, B-4, C-2, D-1

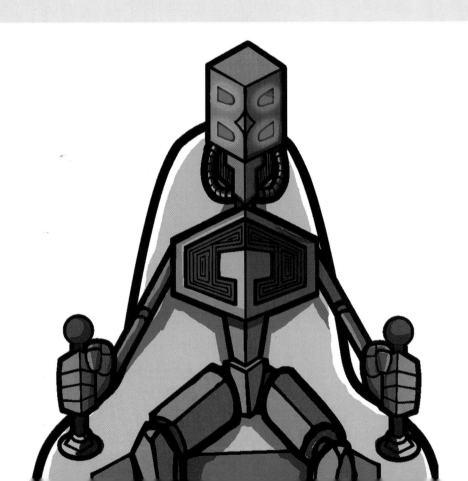

enjoy more of the wonderful world of

Grammar Ray

Grammar Ray
ADJECTIVES

a graphic guide to grammar
andrew carter

ISBN: 9780237538491

Grammar Ray
NOUNS & PRONOUNS

a graphic guide to grammar
andrew carter

ISBN: 9780237537685

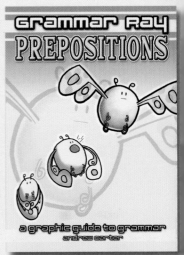

Grammar Ray
PREPOSITIONS

a graphic guide to grammar
andrew carter

ISBN: 9780237538514

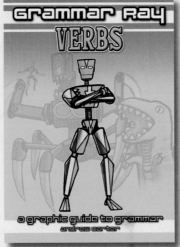

Grammar Ray
VERBS

a graphic guide to grammar
andrew carter

ISBN: 9780237538484

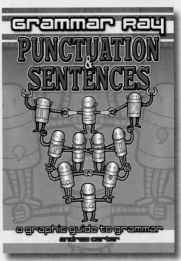

Grammar Ray
PUNCTUATION & SENTENCES

a graphic guide to grammar
andrew carter

ISBN: 9780237538521